Redwork
•Winter Twitterings™•

Designs by Pearl Louise Krush

HOUSE of
WHITE
BIRCHES

PUBLISHERS
SINCE 1947

Introduction

Combine simple embroidery stitches, red embroidery floss, red and white fabrics, and soon you will have created the sweet designs shown on the following pages. Whether you start with the whimsical quilt or try one of the smaller projects first, these twittering friends will be sure to bring a smile to your face as you stitch.

The redwork designs shown in this book can be used for many other projects as well. Simply choose the design and trace it on a white or cream fabric. Then add it to any item of your choice, such as clothing, bags, pillows, pillowcases, etc., to make a creative work of your own.

Hand stitching is a wonderful way to relax the body and soul. Creating fun and functional redwork embroidery projects will bring you hours of fulfilling enjoyment. You'll enjoy making these unique projects to add a special touch to your own home and as gifts for others.

Table of Contents

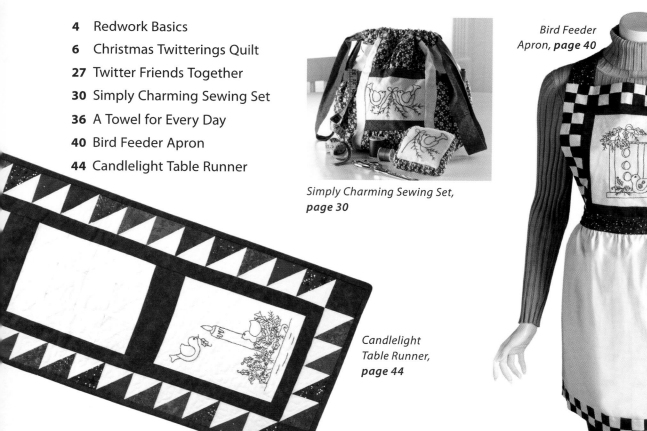

Bird Feeder Apron, page 40

Simply Charming Sewing Set, page 30

Candlelight Table Runner, page 44

Meet the Designer

I simply love to design projects that make people smile. Even as a small child, I enjoyed making things out of paper, clay and fabric.

As a young mother of three sons and the wife of a very busy husband, I wanted to make a little money for all of the extras every family needs. One of the earliest businesses I created was a "Barbie® doll party." I would have my friends and other moms have a Barbie® doll party, and I would show a collection of doll clothes that I had designed. They would order what they wanted, and I would then deliver and charge for the wardrobes that had been ordered. It was a great learning experience.

In 1989, I started the Pearl Louise Designs pattern company and started showing my designs at the International Quilt Market. When my local quilt shop closed, I decided to open The Thimble Cottage Quilt Shop as I needed quilt-shop fabrics to make my designs. The quilt shop and my home are in Rapid City, S.D., just a few miles from Mount Rushmore. During the summer months, we are very busy with visitors from around the world, and I truly enjoy visiting with all of them. Over the years, the shop has evolved into a place where customers can come and enjoy our collection of fabrics, classes and clubs that we offer as well as our Web store, www.thimblecottage.com. I began designing fabric for the Troy Corporation several years ago and have found it very interesting and challenging. Most of my designs are whimsical winter and baby designs, but now I'm venturing into designing a home decor collection, which should be tons of fun.

My husband, Fred, and I enjoy fishing in the summer months. We have two dogs—Bella and Kate, and Telly the bird. Bella goes to the shop every day. My sons are grown, and we now have two wonderful daughters-in-law and three charming grandchildren.

One of my very favorite sayings has always been "Happiness is Homemade."

Enjoy!

Pearl Louise Krush

*A Towel for Every Day, **page 36***

Redwork Basics

Redwork embroidery requires a few supplies and some simple instructions. Read through these basics before you select and begin stitching one of the whimsical projects in this book.

Supplies

Fabric

Use good-quality, 100 percent cotton fabrics in your redwork quilts or projects. The projects in this book were made using white and cream tonals, but any white, off-white or cream high-quality cotton fabric can be used.

Pre-washing your fabrics is recommended, but not absolutely necessary. If you choose not to pre-wash, you must test the fabrics to make sure that they are colorfast and won't shrink.

Start by cutting a 2" by fabric width strip of each fabric you have selected for your redwork project; measure and record the width of each strip.

To determine whether the fabric is colorfast, immerse each strip separately into a clean bowl of extremely hot water, or hold the fabric strip under hot running water. If your fabric bleeds a great deal, all is not necessarily lost. You might be able to wash all of that fabric until all of the excess dye has washed out. Fabrics that continue to bleed after they have been washed several times should be eliminated. You do not want the red fabrics bleeding onto the embroidered squares.

To test for shrinkage, iron each saturated strip dry with a hot iron. When the strip is completely dry, measure and compare the size to the original recorded length. If all of your fabric strips shrink about the same amount, then you have no problem. When you wash your finished quilt or project, you may achieve the puckered look of an antique quilt. If you do not want this look, you will have to wash and dry all fabrics before beginning so that shrinkage is no longer a problem. If one of the fabrics shrinks more than the others, it should be eliminated.

Needles

There are several different types and sizes of needles that can be used for embroidery. Sharps—sizes 7–10—and embroidery needles—sizes 7 and 8 with a longer needle eye for easier threading—are popular. You should choose the size and type of needle you are comfortable with to do your embroidery.

Embroidery Floss

Six-strand cotton embroidery floss was used to embroider the designs in these redwork projects. Work with 1 strand in 18" lengths. You may choose to use 2 strands if you like, especially to stitch the designs on the towels. For the redwork, choose a shade of red such as Anchor 1005 or DMC 498. Be sure the floss you use is guaranteed to be colorfast.

Embroidery Hoops

The best embroidery results are achieved when using an embroidery hoop to hold the fabric taut while stitching. There are several types and sizes of hoops available on the market. Wooden hoops with an adjustable screw are the most common, but there are also spring hoops and the newer Q-snaps. Use the type and size hoop you find most comfortable for embroidering. It is best to use a hoop that is larger than the design you are embroidering, if possible. This helps you avoid having the hoop distort stitches when moved to other areas.

Redwork Embroidery

Tracing the Design

Cut fabric to be embroidered into the size specified with each project's instructions.

Center fabric over the printed design and trace, using a sharp lead pencil or fabric marking pen or pencil. If you use a fabric pen, be sure to follow the manufacturer's directions for proper use. If you cannot see the lines clearly, use a light box for tracing. Remember that the tracing lines should not be visible on the finished project.

Embroidering the Design

Wash your hands before you start hand embroidery to avoid soiling the fabric. Thread floss into needle; do not tie a knot in end.

To begin stitching, come up from the wrong side of the fabric, leaving a 1" tail on the wrong side. Hold the floss end in place so that it is overcast with the first few stitches that are made. Cut the excess floss close to your work when finished.

Another way to begin stitching is to weave floss through several stitches on the wrong side of your work first.

As you embroider separate lines in a close area, it is best to carry the floss across the back as long as the distance is not more than 1". If the lines are more than 1" inch apart, weave the floss through a few stitches on the back side.

Never carry floss across an unworked area. The floss will show through on the finished project.

When finished stitching, weave floss through several stitches on the back side and cut away excess floss.

The Stitches

The stem stitch is the main stitch used to outline redwork designs. To execute the stem stitch, bring the needle up at position A (Figure 1). Hold floss down with the thumb of your non-stitching hand. Reinsert the needle at B and bring up at C, about halfway between A and B. Pull the floss through and continue in this manner with floss held below stitching line and working from left to right.

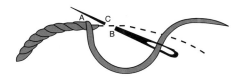

Figure 1

The backstitch may be used to cover right curves and can also be used to outline the designs if desired.

To execute the backstitch, bring needle up at A (Figure 2), a stitch length away from the beginning of the design line. Stitch back down at B, at the beginning of the line, bring needle up at C, and then stitch back down to meet previous stitch at A. Continue in this manner, working in a right-to-left direction.

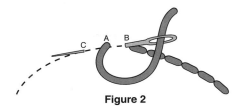

Figure 2

The straight stitch (Figure 3) was used to cover small straight lines. Come up at A and down at B. Straight stitches can be done in varying sizes and spaced regularly or irregularly.

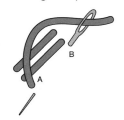

Figure 3

French knots (Figure 4) were used for eyes and any other place where a small dot was needed. Bring needle up at A. Wrap floss once around shaft of needle. Insert point of needle at B (close to, but not into A). Hold knot down as you pull needle through to back of fabric.

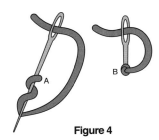

Figure 4

Finishing the Embroidered Block

When embroidery is completed, you may wash in cool water if soiled. To press, place block face down on a hard, padded surface (ironing board with terry towel works fine); press carefully.

Trim block to measurement specified in individual project instructions, being sure to center the design. To do this, find the approximate center of the design and measure an equal distance to all four sides. For example, if the block is to be cut at 6½" x 6½", measure 3¼" from the center point to each side and trim. A wide acrylic ruler and a rotary cutter will aid in measuring and cutting. ❖

Christmas Twitterings Quilt

This whimsical quilt is filled with redwork motifs that will delight you and your friends when the project is hanging in your home.

Project Specifications
Skill Level: Intermediate
Quilt Size: 36" x 44"
Block Sizes: 3" x 3", 4" x 4", 10" x 6", 8" x 10",
6" x 6", 6" x 9", 6" x 4" and 6" x 8"
Number of Blocks: 6, 36, 1, 2, 2, 2, 2 and 3

Materials
- ⅛ yard 1 red/burgundy tonal
- 6 different red/burgundy fat quarters
- 5 different white/cream fat quarters
- 1 dark cream tonal fat quarter
- ¼ yard red tonal for border
- ½ yard burgundy tonal for binding
- ½ yard each 5 white/cream tonals for embroidery
- Batting 44" x 52"
- Backing 44" x 52"
- All-purpose thread to match fabrics
- Quilting thread
- Red embroidery floss
- Large-eye embroidery needle
- Basic sewing tools and supplies

Birds on Chalet
6" x 8" Block
Make 1

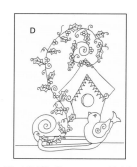

Bird & Birdhouse on Table
6" x 8" Block
Make 1

Tree
6" x 9" Block
Make 1

Birds & Candle
6" x 9" Block
Make 1

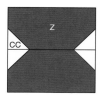

Connector
4" x 4" Block
Make 18

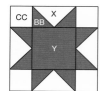

Star
4" x 4" Block
Make 18

Pinwheel
3" x 3" Block
Make 6

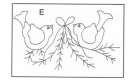

Birds & Twigs
6" x 4" Block
Make 1

Bird & Pinecone
6" x 4" Block
Make 1

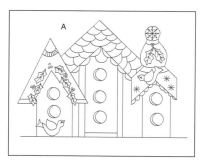

Birdhouses
10" x 8" Block
Make 1

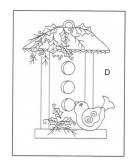

Bird & Bird Feeder
6" x 8" Block
Make 1

Snowman
8" x 10" Block
Make 1

8

Birds on Wreath
6" x 6" Block
Make 1

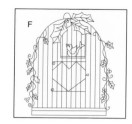

Bird Cage
6" x 6" Block
Make 1

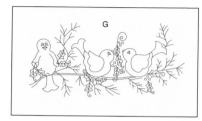

Birds on Twig
10" x 6" Block
Make 1

Completing the Redwork Embroidery

Note: The redwork embroidery is completed on the white/cream yardage before cutting any of the pieces to allow for making the best use of the fabric.

1. Press each white/cream half-yard piece.

2. Mark an embroidery design on one ½-yard fabric piece, beginning 4" from each edge of the fabric and referring to Redwork Basics on page 4 and Figure 1. Mark additional designs on the same fabric, leaving at least 8" between each design, again referring to Figure 1. *Note: The remainder of the yardage will be used to cut other pieces later, so it is important to place the design to make the best use of the fabric and still allow excess space all around for trimming to size after embroidery is complete.*

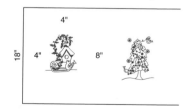

Figure 1

3. Repeat step 2 on the remaining half-yard pieces to transfer all designs.

4. Complete the redwork embroidery on all marked pieces, referring to Redwork Basics on page 4.

5. Trim the embroidered designs to the following sizes: A (Snowman and Birdhouses) 8½" x 10½";

D (Bird & Birdhouse on Table, Bird & Birdfeeder and Birds on Chalet) 6½" x 8½"; E (Bird & Pinecone and Birds & Twigs) 6½" x 4½"; F (Bird Houses, Birds on Wreath and Bird Cage) 6½" x 6½"; G (Birds on Twig) 6½" x 10½"; and DD (Birds & Candle and Tree) 6½" x 9½".

6. Remove transfer marks, if necessary.

Cutting

1. Cut two 1⅞" x 21" strips from one white/cream fat quarter; subcut strips into (16) 1⅞" Q squares.

2. Cut two 2⅜" x 21" strips from the same white/cream fat quarter; subcut strips into (12) 2⅜" H squares.

3. Cut one 1½" x 21" L strip from the same white/cream fat quarter.

4. Cut one 3¼" x 21" strip from the same white/cream fat quarter; subcut strip into six 3¼" S squares.

5. Cut three 1½" x 21" strips from the dark cream fat quarter; subcut strips into two each 8½" B and 12½" C strips and four 1" x 3½" AA strips.

6. Cut one 1½" x 21" strip from the remaining white/cream/dark cream fabrics (fat quarters or yardage); subcut the strip into one matching set of four 1½" x 1½" CC squares and four 1½" x 2½" X rectangles. Repeat to cut a total of 18 sets of CC and X rectangles for Star blocks.

7. Repeat step 6 to cut 18 sets of four 1½" x 1½" CC squares for Connector blocks.

8. Cut two 1⅞" x 21" strips from one red/burgundy fat quarter; subcut strips into (16) 1⅞" R squares.

9. Cut two 2⅜" x 21" strips from the same red/burgundy fat quarter; subcut strips into (12) 2⅜" I squares.

10. Cut one 1½" x 21" M strip from the same red/burgundy fat quarter.

11. Cut one 3¼" x 21" strip from the same red/burgundy fat quarter; subcut strip into six 3¼" T squares.

12. Cut two 1½" x 26½" V strips and two 1½" x 36½" W strips red tonal.

13. Cut four 2½" by fabric width strips burgundy tonal for binding.

14. Cut six 1½" x 21" strips from the remaining red/burgundy fabrics (yardage and fat quarters); subcut strips into two 10½" J strips, two 17½" K strips, two 7½" N strips, three 6½" P strips and two 2½" U strips.

15. Cut one 2½" x 21" strip from the remaining red/burgundy fabrics; subcut the strip into one matching set of one 2½" Y square and eight 1½" x 1½" BB squares. Repeat to cut a total of 18 sets of Y and BB squares for Star blocks.

16. Cut one matching set of two 2½" x 4½" Z rectangles from remaining red/burgundy fabrics. Repeat to cut a total of 18 sets of Z rectangles for Connector blocks.

17. Cut two 1" x 6½" O strips from the remaining red/burgundy fabrics.

Completing the Four-Patch Units

1. Select the 1½" x 21" L and M strips; join with right sides together along length to make an L-M strip set. Press seam toward M.

2. Subcut the L-M strip set into eight 1½" L-M units as shown in Figure 2.

Figure 2   **Figure 3**

3. Join two L-M units as shown in Figure 3 to complete a Four-Patch unit; press seam in one direction. Repeat to make a total of four Four-Patch units.

Completing the Pinwheel Blocks

1. Draw a diagonal line from corner to corner on the wrong side of each H square.

2. Place an H square right sides together with an I square; stitch ¼" on each side of the marked line, referring to Figure 4. Cut apart on the marked line and press I to the right side to complete two H-I units, again referring to Figure 4. Repeat to make a total of 24 H-I units.

Figure 4

3. Join four H-I units as shown in Figure 5 to complete one Pinwheel block; press seam in one direction. Repeat to make a total of six Pinwheel blocks.

Figure 5

Completing the Star Blocks

1. Draw a diagonal line from corner to corner on the wrong side of all BB squares.

2. To complete one Star block, select eight BB squares and one Y square from one red fabric and four CC squares and four X rectangles from one white/cream fabric.

3. Place a BB square on one end of one X rectangle and stitch on the marked line as shown in Figure 6; trim seam to ¼" and press BB to the right side, again referring to Figure 6.

Figure 6   **Figure 7**

4. Repeat step 3 with BB on the opposite end of X to complete a BB-X unit as shown in Figure 7.

5. Repeat steps 3 and 4 to make a total of four BB-X units

6. Sew a BB-X unit to opposite sides of Y as shown in Figure 8; press seams toward Y.

Figure 8   **Figure 9**

7. Sew a CC square to each end of each remaining BB-X unit to complete a BB-CC-X row as shown in Figure 9; press seams toward CC.

8. Sew a BB-CC-X row to opposite sides of the BB-X-Y row to complete one Star block, referring to Figure 10; press seams in one direction.

Figure 10

9. Repeat Steps 2–8 to complete a total of 18 Star blocks.

Completing the Connector Blocks

1. Draw a diagonal line from corner to corner on the wrong side of all remaining CC squares.

2. Select two matching Z rectangles and four matching CC squares.

3. Sew the CC squares to two opposite corners of Z as in steps 3 and 4 in Completing the Star Blocks and referring to Figure 11 to complete a CC-Z unit.

Figure 11

4. Repeat steps 2 and 3 to make a total of 36 CC-Z units.

5. Select two matching CC-Z units and join as shown in Figure 12, to complete one Connector block; press seam in one direction. Repeat to make a total of 18 Connector blocks.

Figure 12

Completing the S-T Sashing Strips

1. Draw a diagonal line from corner to corner on the wrong side of each S square.

2. Place a marked S square right sides together with a T square and sew ¼" on each side of the marked line as shown in Figure 13; cut apart on the marked line, open and press with seam toward T. Repeat with all S and T squares to make a total of 12 units.

Figure 13   **Figure 14**

3. Place two units right sides together with opposite fabrics touching as shown in Figure 14; draw a diagonal line from corner to corner on the top unit across the previous seam, again referring to Figure 14.

4. Sew ¼" on each side of the marked line as shown in Figure 15; cut apart on the marked line and press units open to reveal two S-T units, again referring to Figure 15.

Figure 15

5. Repeat steps 2–4 to complete a total of 12 S-T units.

6. Join three S-T units to make an S-T sashing strip as shown in Figure 16; press seams in one direction. Repeat to make a total of four S-T sashing strips.

Figure 16

Completing the Q-R Sashing Strips

1. Draw a diagonal line from corner to corner on the wrong side of each Q square.

2. Place a marked Q square right sides together with an R square; stitch ¼" on each side of the marked line as shown in Figure 17; cut apart on the marked line and press open with seam toward R to complete one Q-R unit, again referring to Figure 17.

Figure 17

3. Repeat step 2 to complete a total of 32 Q-R units.

4. Join 16 Q-R units to make a Q-R sashing strip as shown in Figure 18; press seams in one direction. Repeat to make two Q-R sashing strips.

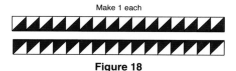

Figure 18

Completing the Quilt

1. Sew B to the top and bottom and C to opposite long sides of the Snowman block; press seams toward B and C strips.

2. Join three Pinwheel blocks with two AA strips to make a pinwheel row as shown in Figure 19; press seam toward AA strips. Repeat to make two pinwheel rows.

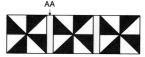

Figure 19

3. Sew a pinwheel row to the top and bottom of the center A-B-C unit; press seams away from the pinwheel row.

4. Sew J to the top and bottom of the pieced unit and add the Birds on Twig block and Birdhouses block to complete the center vertical row as shown in Figure 20; press seams toward J strips.

Figure 20

5. Sew a Four-Patch unit to one end of two S-T rows to make S-T/Four-Patch rows as shown in Figure 21; press seams toward the Four-Patch units. Repeat with the remaining S-T rows, adding a U piece to the opposite end of each row to make two S-T-U/Four-Patch rows, again referring to Figure 21; press seams away from the S-T rows.

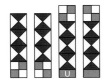

Figure 21

6. Sew an S-T/Four-Patch row to the right-side edge of the Birds on Chalet block and the left-side edge of the Bird & Bird Feeder block as shown in Figure 22; press seams toward the blocks.

Figure 22

7. Repeat step 6 with an S-T-U/Four-Patch row on the right-side edge of the Birds & Candle block and the left-side edge of the Tree block, again referring to Figure 22.

8. Sew a P strip to the bottom of the Birds on Wreath and Bird & Birdhouse on Table blocks; press seams toward P strips.

9. Join the two bordered blocks and add a Q-R strip to the left-side edge, an N strip to the top and a K strip to the right-side edge to complete the left-side strip, referring to Figure 23; press seams toward the N, Q-R and K strips.

10. Join the bordered units, again referring to Figure 23 to complete the left-side row; press seams toward N and P strips.

11. Sew the left-side row to the left side of the center row; press seams toward left-side row.

12. Sew an S-T/Four-Patch row to the left-side edge of the Bird & Bird Feeder block, again referring to Figure 22; press seams toward the blocks.

13. Repeat step 6 with an S-T-U/Four-Patch row on the left-side edge of the Tree block, again referring to Figure 22.

14. Join the Bird & Pinecone, Bird Cage and Bird & Twigs blocks with O and P strips, again referring to Figure 23; press seams toward O and P strips.

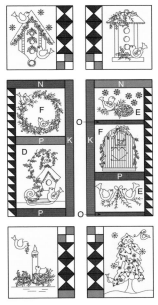

Figure 23

15. Sew the remaining Q-R strip to the right-side edge of the pieced unit, again referring to Figure 23; add N to the top and K to the left-side edge. Press seams toward N and K strips.

16. Join the units to complete the right-side row, again referring to Figure 23; press seams toward N and O strips.

17. Sew the right-side row to the right-side edge of the pieced center row to complete the quilt center; press seams toward the right-side row.

18. Sew the V strips to the top and bottom and W strips to opposite long sides of the pieced center; press seams toward V and W strips.

19. Join four Star blocks with five Connector blocks to make a side row as shown in Figure 24; press seams toward the Star blocks. Repeat to make two side rows.

Figure 24

20. Sew a side row to opposite long sides of the pieced center; press seams toward the W strips.

21. Join four Connector blocks with five Star blocks to make a row; repeat to make two rows. Press seams toward Connector blocks.

22. Sew these rows to the top and bottom of the pieced center to complete the pieced top; press seams toward V strips.

Completing the Quilt

1. Sandwich the batting between the completed top and prepared backing; pin or baste layers together.

2. Quilt as desired by hand or machine. When quilting is complete, trim batting and backing even with edges of the quilted top.

3. Join binding strips on short ends with diagonal seams to make one long strip; trim seams to ¼" and press seams open.

4. Fold binding strip in half wrong sides together along length; press.

5. Sew binding to the right side of the pieced top, matching raw edges, mitering corners and overlapping ends; press binding away from quilt edges and turn to the back side. Hand- or machine-stitch in place. ❖

Christmas Twitterings Quilt
Placement Diagram 36" x 44"

Bird & Bird Feeder Embroidery Design

Snowman Embroidery Design

Bird & Birdhouse on Table Embroidery Design

Birds on Chalet Embroidery Design

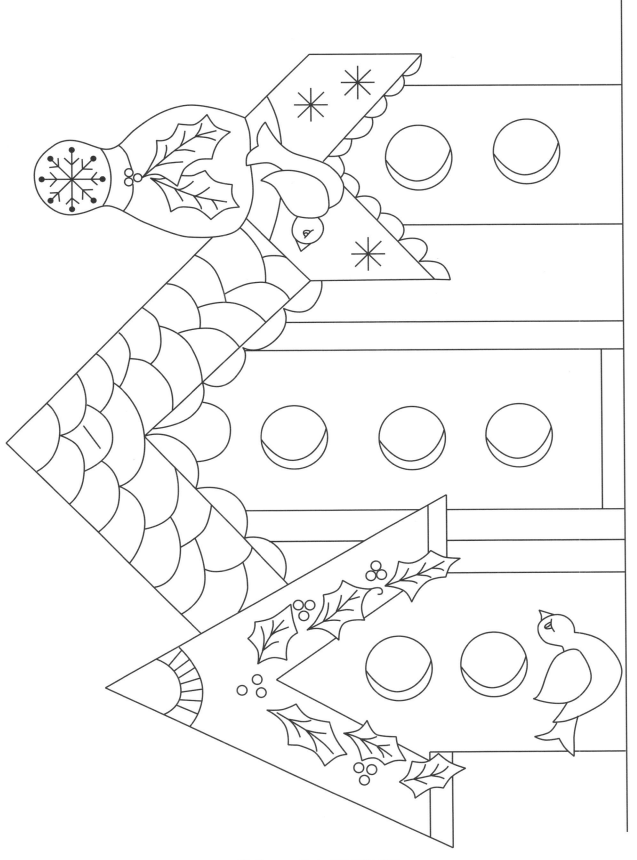

Birdhouses Embroidery Design

House of White Birches, Berne, Indiana 46711   Clotilde.com

Birds & Candle Embroidery Design

Tree Embroidery Design

Birds & Twigs Embroidery Design

Bird & Pinecone Embroidery Design

House of White Birches, Berne, Indiana 46711   Clotilde.com

Birds on Wreath Embroidery Design

Bird Cage Embroidery Design

House of White Birches, Berne, Indiana 46711 Clotilde.com

Birds on Twig Embroidery Design

Twitter Friends Together

Display this charming pillow on a bed, bookcase, dresser or next to the darling framed Snowman. It will add a touch of whimsy no matter where you place it.

Twitter Friends Together Pillow

Project Specifications
Skill Level: Beginner
Pillow Size: 10" x 7"

Materials
- ⅛ yard dark red mottled
- ½ yard white tonal
- Red embroidery floss
- Large-eye embroidery needle
- Polyester fiberfill
- 4 (½") mother-of-pearl buttons
- Basic sewing tools and supplies

Cutting
1. Cut two 12" x 12" squares white tonal.

2. Cut two 11½" x 7½" rectangles white tonal.

3. Cut one 1½" by fabric width strip dark red mottled.

Completing the Redwork Embroidery
1. Fold and crease one 12" x 12" square white tonal to mark the horizontal and vertical centers.

2. Trace the Birds on Twig redwork design given on page 26 onto the square and complete the embroidery, referring to Redwork Basics on page 4.

3. Remove transfer marks, if necessary.

Completing the Pillow
1. Sandwich the batting between the remaining 12" x 12" white square and the stitched redwork square; pin or baste to hold.

2. Quilt as desired by hand or machine; remove pins or basting. *Note: Quilting can be confined to a 10½" x 7½" area.*

3. Trim the quilted square to 10½" x 7½" with stitched design centered.

4. Fold the 1½" by fabric width strip in half with wrong sides together along length; press.

5. Pin the raw edges of the folded strip to the outer raw edges of the quilted pillow top, trim to fit,

extending ¼" on each end. Unpin and unfold ends enough to allow stitching and join the short ends of the strip. Refold and re-pin to the pillow top; stitch all around.

6. Fold each 11½" x 7½" white rectangle in half with wrong sides together to make two 5¾" x 7½" rectangles; press.

7. Pin the two folded rectangles right sides together with the quilted pillow top, overlapping the folded edges as shown in Figure 1; baste overlapped area at outer edges together to hold.

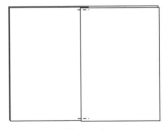

Figure 1

8. Stitch all around pillow edges; trim corners.

9. Turn right side out through opening on the back side; press flat.

10. Insert polyester fiberfill inside pillow through back opening to desired fullness. Hand-stitch overlapped edges together.

11. Stitch a button to each corner of the pillow top to finish.

Twitter Friends Together Framed Picture

Project Specifications
Skill Level: Beginner
Framed Picture Size: 8" x 10"

Materials
- 2 fat quarters white tonal
- Red embroidery floss
- Large-eye embroidery needle
- Easel-back frame with 8" x 10" opening
- Wide, clear tape or masking tape
- Basic sewing tools and supplies

Cutting
1. Fold and crease one white tonal fat quarter to mark the center.

2. Center and trace the Snowman redwork design given on page 14 onto the creased fat quarter and complete the redwork embroidery, referring to Redwork Basics on page 4.

3. Remove transfer marks, if necessary.

Framing the Stitched Design
1. Press the stitched design.

2. Place the second fat quarter wrong sides together with the stitched design; press.

3. Center the layered, stitched design right side up on the cardboard insert from the picture frame; turn over and pull fabric edges tightly over the cardboard from the front side to the back side, stretching to make a tight fit.

4. Using wide tape, tape the edges in place on the cardboard to hold taut.

5. Insert the stitched design in the frame to finish. ❖

Twitter Friends Together Framed Picture
Placement Diagram 8" x 10"

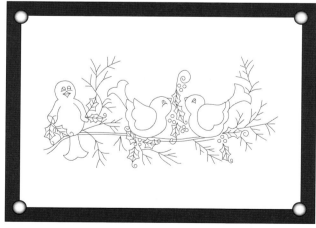

Twitter Friends Together Pillow
Placement Diagram 10" x 7"

Simply Charming Sewing Set

This sewing bag has pockets to hold all the tools you will need to take your stitching projects to any class, appointment or somewhere just for fun. The matching pincushion is the perfect size to hold all of those embroidery or sewing needles and pins.

Sewing Bag

Project Specifications
Skill Level: Intermediate
Bag Size: 16½" x 12"

Materials
- ½ yard red tonal
- ½ yard cream print
- ½ yard white/cream tonal
- ⅞ yard red/white print
- All-purpose thread to match fabrics
- Red embroidery floss
- Large-eye embroidery needle
- ¼ yard heavyweight fusible craft interfacing
- 1 (1") white button
- 1 (¾") red button
- 1 (⅜") heart button
- Basic sewing tools and supplies

Cutting
1. Cut one 12½" by fabric width strip white/cream tonal; subcut strip into two 4½" E, four 1½" D and one 15½" I rectangles.

2. Cut two 2½" by fabric width strips red/white print; subcut strips into two 18" H strips and two 17½" M strips.

3. Cut one 3½" by fabric width strip red/white print; subcut strip into two 3½" x 9½" C rectangles.

4. Cut two 8½" by fabric width strip red/white print; subcut strip into two 7½" G and two 24½" K rectangles.

5. Cut one 12½" x 33½" lining rectangle from cream print.

6. Cut one 1½" by fabric width strip red tonal; subcut strip into two 6½" B strips.

7. Cut one 2½" by fabric width strip red tonal; subcut strip into one 15½" J and two 4½" F rectangles.

8. Cut two 4½" by fabric width N strips red tonal.

9. Prepare template for L using pattern given; cut as directed on the pattern.

Completing the Redwork Embroidery
1. Trace and stitch the Birds & Twigs design given on page 22 onto the leftover white/cream tonal, referring to Redwork Basics on page 4.

2. Center and trim the embroidered design to 6½" x 4½" for A.

3. Remove transfer marks, if necessary.

Completing Side 1
1. Sew two rows of gathering stitches on both 7½" edges of each G rectangle. Repeat on one 9½" edge of the C rectangles.

2. Pull the bobbin threads on the G rectangles so G measures 4½" on each end for the side pockets.

3. Repeat step 3 with C to measure 6½".

4. Sew a B strip to the top and bottom of the embroidered A rectangle; press seams toward B.

5. Pin and stitch the gathered edges of the C rectangles to the B sides of the stitched A-B unit to complete the center A-B-C panel as shown in Figure 1; press seams toward B strips.

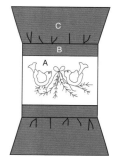

Figure 1

6. Sew an F strip to one 4½" edge of each gathered G piece as shown in Figure 2; fold the remaining long raw edge of F ¼" to the wrong side and press.

Figure 2 **Figure 3**

7. Fold F to the wrong side of G to cover the F-G seam as shown in Figure 3; hand- or machine-stitch in place to complete one side pocket. Repeat to make two side pockets.

8. Measure up 1" on one end of each E rectangle and mark a line as shown in Figure 4.

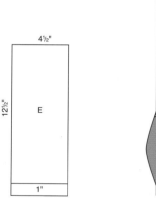

Figure 4 **Figure 5**

9. Place the remaining gathered edge of one side pocket right sides together, aligning the raw edge of G on the marked line on E as shown in Figure 5; stitch with a ¼" seam. Press the side pocket to the right side onto the upper part of E and baste side edges to hold, as shown in Figure 6, to complete a side pocket. Repeat to make a second side pocket.

Figure 6

10. Sew a D strip to each long side of the center panel; press seams toward D strips.

11. Sew a side pocket to the remaining sides of D as shown in Figure 7; press seams toward D.

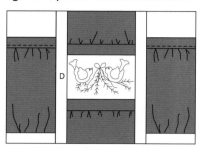

Figure 7

12. Sew a D strip to each end of the pieced unit to complete side 1 of the bag as shown in Figure 8; press seams toward D strips.

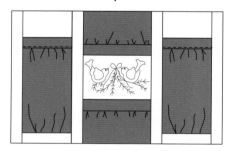

Figure 8

Completing Side 2

1. Sew two rows of gathering stitches on both 24½" edges of the K rectangle. Pull bobbin threads to gather each edge to make 15½" long.

2. Sew the J strip to one gathered edge of K; fold the remaining long raw edge of J ¼" to the wrong side and press.

3. Fold J to the wrong side of K to cover the J-K seam; hand- or machine-stitch in place.

4. Measure up 1" on one 15½" edge of I and mark a line.

5. Place the remaining gathered edge of K right sides together, aligning the raw edge of K on the marked line on I; stitch with a ¼" seam. Press the J-K unit to the right side onto the upper part of I and baste side edges to hold to complete side 2 as shown in Figure 9.

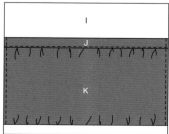

Figure 9

Completing the Bag

1. Sew side 1 to side 2 along the remaining long raw edges of D to complete the body of the bag; press seams toward D.

2. Sew two lines of gathering stitches all the way around the bottom edge of the bag body; pull bobbin threads to gather to fit around the red/white print L piece, matching the center of each side of the bag with the notched centers on L; stitch the bag bottom to L to complete the outside of the bag.

3. Sew the lining rectangle right sides together to make a 12½" x 17" rectangle; press to crease the folded edge to mark the center.

4. Stitch along the 12½" edge to make a tube. Press seam to one side.

5. Fuse the heavyweight craft interfacing to the wrong side of the cream print L.

6. Sew two lines of gathering stitches along the 33½" edge; pull bobbin threads to gather to fit the fused L lining piece. Stitch to hold to complete the bag lining.

7. Insert the lining inside the bag with wrong sides together with seam centered on one side of L and the creased line on the other side of L.

8. Align top edges; baste to hold, except leave the C piece area unstitched.

9. Join the two H strips along one long edge; press seam to one side. Press each short end to the wrong side ¼" and ¼" again and stitch to hem. Press ¼" to the wrong side on one long edge of joined H strips.

10. Repeat step 9 with the two M strips.

11. Sew two lines of gathering stitches along the raw edge of the top center C piece on side 1 as shown in Figure 10. Pull bobbin threads to gather.

Figure 10

12. Center and pin the raw edge of the stitched H strip to side 1, extending ends of H onto the D side strips, as shown in Figure 11, and adjusting the gathers on C to make side 1 fit H; stitch H to the top edge of side 1.

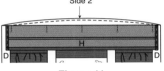

Figure 11

13. Repeat step 12 with the stitched M strip, overlapping H ¼" on each end as shown in Figure 12.

Figure 12

14. Fold the H and M strips to the lining side to cover seam; stitch in place through all layers to complete the casing. Press.

15. Fold each end of one N strip to the wrong side ¼" and press. Fold under ¼" again, press and stitch to hem.

16. Stitch each N strip with right sides together along the length; turn right side out. Press with seam centered on one side.

17. Thread an N strip through the H casing, evenly distributing excess at each end as shown in Figure 13. Repeat with the remaining N strip through the M casing.

Figure 13

18. Insert the raw ends of the unhemmed N strip inside the ends of the hemmed N strip and stitch to complete the bag ties. Pull ties to close bag.

19. Stack the three buttons with largest on the bottom and smallest on top; sew together.

20. Center the button stack on the J strip on side 2 and stitch to bag through all layers to finish.

Sewing Bag
Placement Diagram 16½" x 12"

Pincushion

Project Specifications
Skill Level: Beginner
Pincushion Size: 4" x 4"

Materials
- 1 fat eighth white/cream tonal
- ⅛ yard red/white print
- Red all-purpose thread
- Red embroidery floss
- Large-eye embroidery needle
- Scraps fiberfill
- Basic sewing tools and supplies

Completing the Redwork Embroidery
1. Center, trace and stitch the Bird & Bow design on next page onto the fat eighth white/cream tonal, referring to Redwork Basics on page 4.

2. Center and trim the embroidered design to 4½" x 4½" for A.

Cutting
1. Cut one 4½" x 4½" B square white/cream tonal.

2. Cut one 2" by fabric width C strip red/white print.

Completing the Pincushion
1. Join the short ends of the C strip to make a tube; press seam open.

2. Stitch two rows of gathering stitches on each raw edge of the C tube.

3. Pull the bobbin threads to gather until the strip fits around all sides of the A square.

4. With right sides together, pin one gathered edge of the C tube around the raw edges of A; adjust gathers to fit and stitch.

5. Repeat steps 3 and 4 with the B square and the remaining gathered edge of C, leaving a 2" opening on one side.

6. Insert polyester fiberfill through the opening until firmly stuffed; when satisfied with firmness, hand-stitch the opening closed to finish the pincushion. ❖

Pincushion
Placement Diagram 4" x 4"

Bird & Bow Embroidery Design

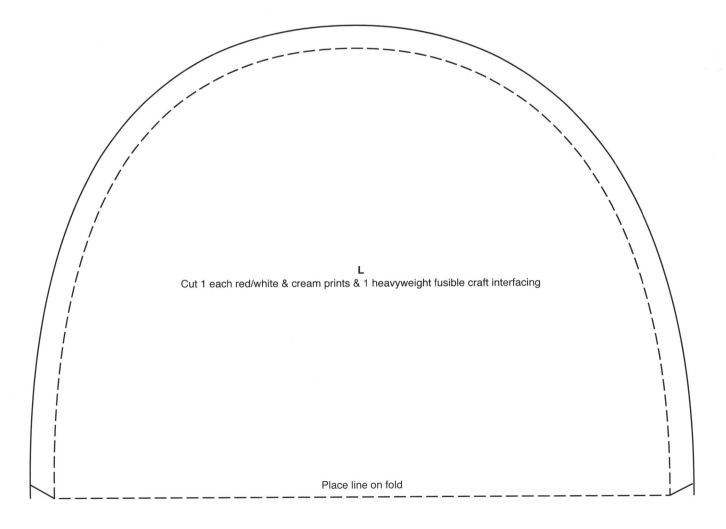

L
Cut 1 each red/white & cream prints & 1 heavyweight fusible craft interfacing

Place line on fold

House of White Birches, Berne, Indiana 46711   Clotilde.com

A Towel for Every Day

Having kitchen towels hanging in your kitchen are great for decorating, but also are very functional. Stitch up a set for your home or as a gift for a friend or family member.

Project Specifications
Skill Level: Beginner
Towel Size: Size Varies

Materials
- 7 cotton dish towels
- Red embroidery floss
- Large-eye embroidery needle
- Basic sewing tools and supplies

Completing the Redwork Embroidery
1. Fold and crease each dish towel on one diagonal to mark the center.

2. Trace a day-of-the-week embroidery design approximately 4" from the corner and 3" from side edges using patterns given on pages 38 and 39, and referring to Figure 1 and the Redwork Basics on page 4.

Figure 1

3. Complete the redwork embroidery on all marked pieces, referring to the Redwork Basics on page 4.

4. Remove transfer marks, if necessary, to complete the tea towels. ❖

Sunday Bird
Placement Diagram Size Varies

Monday Bird
Placement Diagram Size Varies

Tuesday Bird
Placement Diagram Size Varies

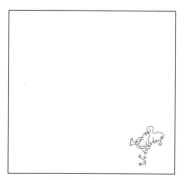

Wednesday Bird
Placement Diagram Size Varies

Thursday Bird
Placement Diagram Size Varies

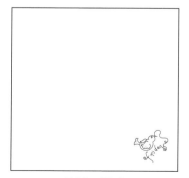

Friday Bird
Placement Diagram Size Varies

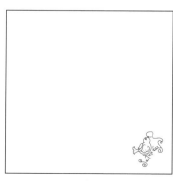

Saturday Bird
Placement Diagram Size Varies

Sunday Bird Embroidery Design

Monday Bird Embroidery Design

Tuesday Bird Embroidery Design

Wednesday Bird Embroidery Design

Thursday Bird Embroidery Design

Friday Bird Embroidery Design

Saturday Bird Embroidery Design

House of White Birches, Berne, Indiana 46711   Clotilde.com

Bird Feeder Apron

Aprons are in, and this apron is another functional item needed in every kitchen. You will look fantastic when you wear this charming stitched apron.

Project Specifications
Skill Level: Intermediate
Apron Size: One size fits most

Materials
- ¼ yard dark red mottled
- ½ yard dark red print
- 1½ yards white/cream tonal
- Red embroidery floss
- Large-eye embroidery needle
- Basic sewing tools and supplies

Cutting
1. Cut one 12½" by fabric width strip white/cream tonal; subcut strip into one 29" rectangle for embroidery and one 12½" square for bib lining.

2. Cut one 27½" by fabric width strip white/cream tonal; subcut strip into one 18½" F rectangle and one 20½" skirt lining rectangle.

3. Cut three 1½" by fabric width D strips white/cream tonal.

4. Cut one 5½" x 6½" pocket lining rectangle from white/cream tonal.

5. Cut one 2½" by fabric width strip dark red print; subcut strip into two 20½" G strips.

6. Cut two 5" by fabric width strips dark red print; subcut strip into three 20" H strips.

7. Cut four 1½" by fabric width strips dark red mottled; subcut one strip into four 8½" B strips. Set aside remaining strips for E.

Completing the Redwork Embroidery
1. Center and trace the complete Bird & Bird Feeder design given on page 13, starting 4" from one end of the 12½"-wide white/cream strip and referring to Redwork Basics on page 4. Measure 8" from the traced design and trace the bird and twig section only of the design in the center of the strip as shown in Figure 1.

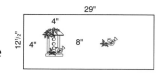
Figure 1

2. Trim excess strip 4" from the traced design to reduce bulk, if necessary.

3. Complete the redwork embroidery, referring to Redwork Basics on page 4.

4. Remove transfer marks if necessary.

5. Fold and crease the embroidered motifs on the strip both horizontally and vertically. Center and trim the Bird & Bird Feeder design to 6½" x 8½" for A. Repeat with the bird and twig motif to cut a 5½" x 4½" C pocket, referring to Figure 2.

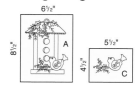
Figure 2

Completing the Apron
1. Sew a B strip to opposite long sides and to the top and bottom of the embroidered A rectangle; press seams toward B strips.

2. Sew a D strip to an E strip along length to make a D-E strip set; press seam toward D strip. Repeat to make a total of three D-E strip sets.

3. Subcut the D-E strip sets into (64) 1½" D-E units as shown in Figure 3.

Figure 3

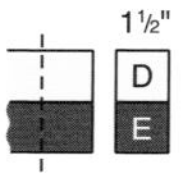

4. Join 10 D-E units to make a side strip as shown in Figure 4; press seams in one direction. Repeat to make a second side strip.

Figure 4

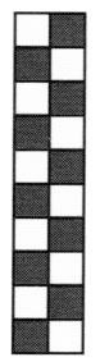

5. Sew a side strip to opposite sides of the A-B unit; press seams toward B strips.

6. Join 12 D-E units to make a top strip; press seams in one direction.

7. Sew the top strip to the top of the bordered A-B unit to complete the apron bib as shown in Figure 5.

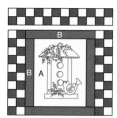

Figure 5

8. Join five D-E units to make a pocket strip; press seams in one direction.

9. Sew the pocket strip to the top edge of the embroidered C rectangle, referring to Figure 6; press seam toward C.

Figure 6

10. Place the 5½" x 6½" pocket lining piece right sides together with the bordered C piece; stitch all around, leaving a 3" opening on one side.

11. Trim corners and turn right side out through the opening; press edges flat. Turn opening edges in ¼"; hand-stitch closed.

12. Topstitch ⅛" from the edge around the three sides of the pocket.

13. Place and pin the pocket to the F apron piece 6¼" from one 18" side edge and 3½" from the 27½" top edge as shown in Figure 7; stitch in place over the previous topstitching.

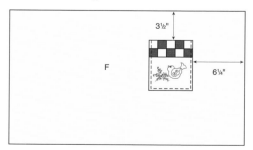

Figure 7

14. Join 27 D-E units to make the bottom strip; press seams in one direction.

15. Sew the pieced strip to the bottom 27½" edge of the F piece to complete the apron skirt as shown in Figure 8.

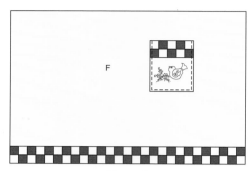

Figure 8

16. Place the skirt lining right sides together with the pieced apron skirt; stitch together at side and bottom edges, leaving the top edge open.

17. Turn the stitched skirt right side out and press edges flat; pin top open edges together.

18. Set sewing machine to a gathering stitch and stitch two lines of gathering stitches across the pinned top edge.

19. Pull bobbin threads to gather to make the top edge 20" long; fold and mark the center of the gathered edge.

20. Repeat steps 16 and 17 with the bib and bib lining pieces, leaving the bottom edge open.

21. Fold the apron bib in half along the length and mark the bottom center with a pin. Repeat with each G strip.

22. Place the two G strips right sides together, insert and center the apron bib between the two strips as shown in Figure 9; stitch.

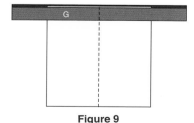

Figure 9

23. Press the G strips away from the apron bib.

24. Center the G/bib unit with the right side of one G strip against the right side of the gathered apron skirt as shown in Figure 10; stitch the unit to the skirt through one G strip. ***Note: Raw edges will extend ¼" beyond skirt edge at each end.***

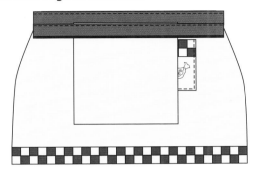

Figure 10

25. Press the long raw edge of the remaining G strip side under ¼"; pin over the seam between the G/bib unit and the skirt to cover the seam. Hand-stitch G in place on the wrong side of the skirt.

26. Fold each H strip with right sides together along length; mark a diagonal line on one end of two of the folded strips as shown in Figure 11. Stitch along the long edges and on the marked diagonal line; trim excess at the diagonal seam to ¼". Turn right side out and press edges flat.

H

Figure 11

27. Pleat the raw end of the stitched strips and insert in the opening at the ends of the G waistband; turn the ends of G ¼" to the inside and machine-stitch to secure ties and to close open ends. ***Note: The diagonal direction of both ties should be the same.***

28. Stitch the remaining H strip along long raw edge; turn right side out and press edges flat. Turn in both ends ¼", press and stitch to finish.

29. Place the ends of the H strip on the back side of the apron bib for neck strap; adjust length to fit. Pin in place.

30. Hand-stitch the strip in place on all sides that touch the bib to finish. ❖

Bird Feeder Apron
Placement Diagram One Size Fits Most

Candlelight Table Runner

Place this sweet table runner on your kitchen or dining table. Add a bouquet or candle sconce to the center panel to complete the table decoration.

Project Specifications
Skill Level: Intermediate
Runner Size: 34" x 12"
Block Size: 6" x 8"
Number of Blocks: 2

Materials
- Scraps white/cream prints or tonals
- Scraps red/burgundy prints or tonals
- ⅓ yard dark red mottled
- ½ yard white tonal
- ¼ yard burgundy mottled
- Batting 42" x 20"
- Backing 42" x 20"
- All-purpose thread to match fabrics
- Quilting thread
- Red embroidery floss
- Large-eye embroidery needle
- Basic sewing tools and supplies

Birds & Candle
6" x 8" Block
Make 2

Completing the Redwork Embroidery
Note: The redwork embroidery is completed before cutting any of the pieces to allow for making best use of the white/cream fat quarters fabrics after trimming the embroidered squares or rectangles from the pieces.

1. Press the half-yard white tonal piece.

2. Mark two Birds & Candle embroidery designs given on page 20 on the white tonal piece leaving at least 4" all around each design and complete the embroidery, referring to Redwork Basics on page 4 and Figure 1.

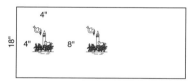

Figure 1

3. Trim the embroidered designs to 6½" x 8½" to complete two Birds & Candle blocks. *Note: These blocks are trimmed smaller than the blocks of the same design in the quilt.*

4. Remove transfer marks, if necessary.

Cutting
1. Cut (12) 3¼" x 3¼" B squares from the white/cream scraps.

2. Cut (19) 2⅞" x 2⅞" D squares from the white/cream scraps.

3. Cut (19) 2⅞" x 2⅞" E squares red/burgundy scraps.

4. Cut one 2½" by fabric width strip burgundy mottled; subcut strip into two 6½" A strips and four 2½" F squares.

5. Cut two 1½" by fabric width strips burgundy mottled; subcut each strip into one each 28½" C strip and 8½" D strip.

6. Cut three 2½" by fabric width strips dark red mottled for binding.

Completing the B Units
1. Draw a diagonal line from corner to corner on the wrong side of six B squares.

2. Place a marked B square right sides together with a B square of a different fabric and sew ¼" on each side of the marked line as shown in Figure 2; cut apart on the marked line, open and press with seam in one direction. Repeat with all B squares to make 12 units.

Figure 2

3. Place two units right sides together with opposite fabrics touching as shown in Figure 3; Draw a diagonal line from corner to corner on the top unit across the previous seam, again referring to Figure 3.

Figure 3

4. Sew ¼" on each side of the marked line as shown in Figure 4; cut apart on the marked line and press units open to reveal two B units, again referring to Figure 4.

Figure 4

5. Repeat steps 3 and 4 to complete a total of 12 B units.

6. Join four B units to make a B row; press seams in one direction. Repeat to make three B rows.

7. Join the B rows to complete the B center unit as shown in Figure 5; press seams in one direction.

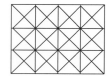

Figure 5

Completing the E-F Units

1. Draw a diagonal line from corner to corner on the wrong side of each F square.

2. Place a marked F square right sides together with an E square; stitch ¼" on each side of the marked line as shown in Figure 6; cut apart on the marked line and press open with seam toward E to complete one E-F unit, again referring to Figure 6.

Figure 6

3. Repeat step 2 to complete a total of 38 E-F units.

4. Join 15 E-F units to make a long E-F border strip as shown in Figure 7; press seams in one direction. Repeat to make two long E-F border strips.

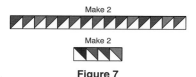

Figure 7

5. Join four E-F units to make a short E-F border strip, again referring to Figure 7; press seams in one direction. Repeat to make two short E-F border strips.

Completing the Top

1. Sew an A strip to opposite short ends of the B center unit; press seams toward A strips.

2. Add an embroidered Birds & Candle block to the remaining sides of A to complete the pieced center; press seams toward A.

3. Sew C strips to opposite long sides and D strips to the short ends of the pieced center; press seams toward C and D strips.

4. Sew a long E-F border strip to opposite long sides of the pieced center; press seam toward C strips.

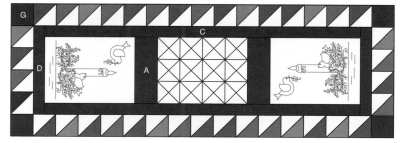

Candlelight Table Runner
Placement Diagram 34" x 12"